The New Wonder of the World.

BUFFALO:

THE ELECTRIC CITY.

By A. E. RICHMOND.

THE MATTHEWS-NORTHRUP CO., COMPLETE ART-PRINTING WORKS,

BUFFALO, N. Y.
14298

Media Hatchery
Orchard Park, NY

ISBN: 978-0-9971276-3-8 (Paperback Edition)

Cover Image:
Labor Day crowd, Main St., Buffalo, N.Y. (c. 1900),
Detroit Publishing Company.
Obtained from the Library of Congress
Prints and Photographs Division.

Printed and bound in the United States of America
First Printing 2021

Published by Media Hatchery
P. O. Box 554
Orchard Park, NY 14127

MediaHatchery.com

~ ~ ~

Other Books on Buffalo from Media Hatchery ...

The River Niagara
by Barton Atkins

Modern Antiquities: Comprising Sketches of Early Buffalo and the Great Lakes | Also Sketches of Alaska
by Barton Atkins

Available from Amazon and Barnes & Noble

WITH COMPLIMENTS OF

THE SECURITY INVESTMENT COMPANY

OF BUFFALO, N. Y.

156 AND 158 PEARL STREET, CORNER CHURCH STREET.

CAPITAL, — — — *$300,000.*

DIRECTORS:

CHARLES A. SWEET, ...	President Third National Bank, Buffalo.
JOHN SATTERFIELD, ...	President Union Oil Company, Buffalo.
EDMUND HAYES, ...	Of the Union Bridge Works, Buffalo.
HON. CHARLES DANIELS, . .	Ex-Judge Supreme Court, Buffalo.
JAMES H. SMITH, ...	Director of the Cary Safe Company, Buffalo.
WALTER G. ROBBINS, ...	Vice-President Buffalo Fish Company, Buffalo.
JAMES R. AUSTIN, ...	Real Estate, Buffalo.
JAMES B. STAFFORD, ...	Real Estate, Buffalo.
RICHARD H. STAFFORD, . . .	Real Estate, Buffalo.
FRANCIS B. THURBER, ...	President Thurber-Whyland Company, wholesale grocers, New York City.
JAMES E. GRANNISS, ...	President The Tradesmen's National Bank, New York City.
JOHN LOUDON, ...	Capitalist, Altoona, Pa.
J. M. GUFFEY, ...	Capitalist, Pittsburg, Pa.

This Company furnishes the investor a safe and reliable channel through which he may place his money. Great care and judgment used before putting an investment on the market. Large and small investors will find it greatly to their advantage to examine the list of investments offered by this Company.

Choice real estate a specialty.

Bonds and mortgages and other first-class securities handled.

THE NIAGARA CATARACT — SOURCE OF BUFFALO'S ELECTRIC POWER.

DEDICATION

To my other amazing son, Joseph. Perhaps one day you will tire of the greener grass of the West Coast and return to Western New York to hang a shingle near the place where you were born.

I'm looking forward to it.

— William C. Even, Media Hatchery

FOREWORD

In 2018 I began to seek out and restore vintage images of Buffalo and Western New York for my website **NostalgicBuffalo.com**. The pursuit of these images led me to the discovery of a handful of fascinating books from the 1890s (now in the public domain) extolling the virtues of Buffalo and Western New York.

Buffalo: The Electric City is the third book that I have selected to restore and republish. It speaks of the incalculable potential of Buffalo and surrounding areas, thanks to "a combination of unlimited cheap power for manufacturing and extraordinary shipping facilities."

For many years (mostly while shoveling snow in February), I have cursed the choices of my ancestors for settling in Western New York instead of somewhere warm like Ft. Lauderdale or San Diego. It was not until I found this book that the rationale for their decisions became clear.

According to his obituary in the Buffalo News, my maternal great-grandfather, John Bianchi (1867-1939), was a "famed sculptor." Born in the village of Pogliana in the Italian-Swiss Alps, great-granddad trained at the Royal Academy of Fine Arts in Milano, where he won the silver medal for first prize in their quinquennial (i.e., every five years) art competition. John then moved to South America to carve fine marble pieces for the homes of presumably wealthy patrons. When yellow fever and revolution broke out, he left for Quincy, MA to work with his cousin at the age of 24.

John returned to Italy in 1894, married Ernestine Nacchi, and returned to the United States to carve friezes for the Library of Congress in Washington, DC. While in DC, his only child, my grandfather Joseph Gabriel Bianchi (1896-1968), was born. The family moved to Buffalo in the late 1890s. In 1906, after working as the superintendent of the **Lautz Marble Works** on Washington Street and at **Bianchi and Abiatti** for several years, John established a family-run monument plant with Joseph — **J. Bianchi and Son, Monuments of Quality** — on Genesee Street in Cheektowaga, very close to the Buffalo border.

What does this have to do with shoveling snow in February? Well, it turns out that in the 1890s (as you will soon discover yourself), Buffalo was becoming a big deal! Shipping was already a major industry here. Now add the harnessing of electric power generated by the Niagara River into the mix — Buffalo was about to explode.

The promise of cheap land and endless, clean, cheap electricity beckoned industrialists and manufacturers from all over. This led to an influx of job-seeking laborers, followed by entrepreneurs that recognized a need for all of the ancillary businesses that sprout up in a growing region.

Where people live, people die. Great-granddad saw an opportunity and set up shop in a thriving metropolis.

And that's why I'm here.

— William C. Even, Media Hatchery

IAGARA'S voice sings a new song.

Through countless ages it has thundered forth its wild, tumultuous melody, a pæan to nature in every tone.

Now it sings an anthem to industry, to science, to inventive genius, to commercial prosperity.

The magic wand of the electrician has been waved, and the mighty voice swells and roars to new music of new and marvelous power.

The new song rising from the mist and the spray of the cataract heralds a new era in Buffalo.

It heralds the evolution of the Queen City of the Lakes into the Electric City of the World; a smokeless, dustless, wholesome city where the myriad and ever-increasing wheels of industry will turn with the silent, unseen power generated from Niagara's unceasing current; a city that will grow and attract and gather force and wealth and people until it comes to be known as *the New Wonder of the World.*

HEN the city of Buffalo, under the favoring conditions which have brought it to its present splendid eminence, doubles its population in ten years, and increases in wealth seven million dollars yearly, what can be foretold of it when in addition to all its present wealth-producing resources it becomes the possessor of an unlimited supply of the cheapest power in the whole world!

Contemplating this fact, the Chicago *Tribune* said: "By virtue of having the cheapest power for turning its machinery, Buffalo will inevitably become the manufacturing centre of the nation."

The New York *Tribune* adds this weighty testimony to the greatness of our future: "The past of Buffalo is secure, and her manifest destiny is evidently to be something tremendous."

Already preparations are being made to bring to Buffalo the electric power from the great tunnel at Niagara Falls. Several companies have been formed of foremost business men, who see that in the distribution and application of the mighty power to industrial uses there are fortunes to be made, and that the pioneers in the task will win the chief prizes.

The time for discussing the practicability of bringing electric power from Niagara Falls to Buffalo has gone by. Electrical science has settled the question completely. It has been demonstrated beyond all question that electric power can be transmitted long distances without material loss.

A number of the greatest capitalists, and shrewdest investors in the United States, are financially interested in the tunnel scheme. Before they put up their money they satisfied themselves not only that the power could be produced, but that it could be sold.

They looked at Buffalo, 22 miles away, and saw a city of nearly 300,000 inhabitants, spread over a large territory, with ample opportunity for territorial growth beyond the present limits, a city in which 3,000 new houses were built in the year 1891, and in which nearly one hundred million dollars is invested in industrial enterprises. They saw a city into which 26 lines of railroad enter, representing a total trackage of about 25,000 miles, and including the great trunk lines leading east, west, north and south, tapping all the rich raw-material storehouses of the continent at all points. They saw that Buffalo had extraordinary facilities for the distribution of manufactures by rail, facilities created by the hand of industry, and they saw too nature's grand gift in the great chain of lakes, coupled to another gift of industry, the Erie canal, giving us a water route to the Atlantic seaboard.

These men saw that here was the place where electric power could be disposed of in enormous quantities. They knew that they could send it here almost as cheaply as they could distribute it in the immediate vicinity of its point of production, and they saw the mighty certainties in a combination of unlimited cheap power for manufacturing and extraordinary shipping facilities. They knew that a market for their electrical product was forever assured, and they planted their millions in the earth and rock of Niagara. Better investment was never made.

Read the names of some of the great financiers engaged in this enterprise: William K. Vanderbilt, Chauncey M. Depew, Drexel, Morgan & Co., August Belmont, Brown Bros. & Co., Isaac N. Seligman, Winslow, Lamer & Co.. Morris K. Jessup and others famous in the financial world.

OUR GREAT RAILROAD INTERESTS.

Buffalo is one of the greatest railroad centers in the United States. Its advantages for bringing in raw material cheaply and quickly are unequalled. Its railroad arteries go forth in all directions, reaching the rich mines and fertile fields and levying upon the wealth of all; and for the distribution of manufactured products it occupies a commanding position unexcelled by any city in the country. And to all this must be added its peerless shipping facilities by lake and canal, coupled with the fact of its unique location at the point of transhipment between lake, canal and railroad.

The railroad interests of Buffalo are larger than many residents of the city have any idea of. There are more miles of railroad tracks within the city limits than in any other city in the world. We have 660 miles of them. The railroads own over 3,600 acres of land in the city. Over one-tenth of the general city taxes levied in Buffalo is paid by the railroads. An army of over 20,000 men are steadily employed by the railroads in Buffalo. A great number of them own their own homes. With their families they are numerous enough to make a good-sized city of themselves.

THE LAKE AND ENTRANCE TO THE HARBOR.

New industries are constantly being added to swell the bulk of railroad enterprises here. The locomotive shops of the New York Central &: Hudson River Railroad are among the latest. They will cost half a million dollars to build, and they will be equipped with the highest class of machinery, costing several hundred thousand dollars more. It is the intention within a few years to spend about two million dollars on these shops, making them the largest and best equipped locomotive shops in the United States, rivaling the Altoona shops, now the largest in the world.

The building of the Gould Car Coupler Company's works adds another to the long list of railroad supply shops located here, among which are the Wagner Palace Car Works, Buffalo Car Wheel Works, New York Car Wheel Works, Rood & Brown Car Wheel Works, all employing a large number of men. These are the kind of industries that anchor a city to prosperity forever. All this shows what a railroad center Buffalo is and what splendid facilities we have for receiving and sending by rail.

LAKE AND CANAL.

From statistics of lake commerce, compiled by Charles H. Keep, secretary of the Lake Carriers' Association, of Buffalo, it is learned that 30,299,006 tons of cargo were carried on the great lakes during the year 1890. Mr. Keep figures out that if all this tonnage were loaded into railroad cars of fifteen tons capacity, there would be a string of cars covering 13,466 miles of railroad tracks, or, in other words, four strings of cars from New York to San Francisco and enough left over to run two strings of cars from New York to Chicago. And most of this immense amount of tonnage came to Buffalo, or was shipped from Buffalo.

"During the season of 1890," he continues, "more than nine million tons of ore were moved by the lake route from the vicinity of the mines to the vicinity of the furnaces."

To give further proof of the immense volume of trade flowing to and from Buffalo, here are some comparative figures: During 1890 the amount of tonnage passing through the Suez canal was 6,890,094 tons, compared with 8,454,435 tons passing through the St. Mary's Falls canal, and 21,684,000 tons passing through the Detroit River.

In 1891, from April 1st to December 1st, the grain, including flour, discharged from vessels at the port of Buffalo, reached the stupendous amount of 164,459,720 bushels.

In 1891 the total value of imports to Buffalo by canal was $27,942,213, and the total value of exports by canal the same year was $36,978,035. To handle this great volume of business 1180 boats were in use.

GREAT GRAIN STOREHOUSES.

There are 34 grain elevators in Buffalo, with a total capacity of 15,000,000 bushels, in addition to six floaters and six transfer elevators. These structures have a capacity for transferring 4,000,000 bushels every 24 hours. In 1891 they handled 135,315,510 bushels. Their total value is over $8,000,000. Several new elevators of giant size are planned. Two of them are estimated to cost a million dollars each.

WHERE TRADE CONCENTRATES.

Buffalo's location is unique. It is the stopping off place between distant sections for men, animals, lumber, grain and general merchandise. The incidental business growing out of this fact is enormous. Grain, coal, iron, oil, lumber and other products of this great country gravitate toward Buffalo, and here they are sent to the mills, refineries and factories, or are transferred from boats to cars, or cars to boats, and sent east or west as the case may be.

The grain receipts by lake at this port have more than tripled in the past ten years, reaching nearly 165,000,000 bushels in 1891. These shipments are bound to vastly increase as new stretches of country in the West and Northwest are opened up and tapped by railroad lines. The recent passage of the river and harbor appropriation bill, by which an expenditure of $4,000,000 is authorized in securing a twenty-foot channel for lake navigation, will result in still lower rates and greatly increased shipments by lake. The saving in lake freights over the average railroad rates in 1891 was about $150,000,000.

Many of the largest coal trestles in the world are located here. This is the greatest coal distributing point in the world. Our coal trade is simply enormous. To give an indication of this, it is sufficient to quote the coal shipments by lake alone from Buffalo in 1891. They amounted to 2,365,895 tons, and the shipments by canal and rail were very large. A conservative estimate places the value of property used in the coal trade here at $10,000,000. This estimate, of course, does not include vessels engaged in the coal trade, nor railroad property outside of that actually devoted to the coal business.

The lumber trade here is phenomenally large. This, of course, is to be expected, owing to our location at the foot of the great lakes. The rich lumbering districts bordering upon the lakes are tributary to us, and the consequence is that Buffalo and Tonawanda, which are practically one, receive and distribute immense quantities of lumber. This is, in fact, the greatest distributing point for lumber in the world.

In addition to all this, we have the largest sheep market in the world, one of the largest horse markets in the world, and, next to Chicago, the largest cattle market in the world.

THE WONDER OF THE WORLD.

The facts given above are all drawn from compiled statistics of the city, and all show the splendid foundation that has been built for the vast city of the near future when the electric elixir from Niagara's mighty power flows through all our commercial veins and arteries, cheapening the cost of production so that outside competition can be defied, building up every established enterprise, bringing numberless new ones into life, and making of Buffalo the Manchester of the new world! More than that, it will be the wonder of the world, the peerless, marvelous electric city!

All this is coming. There is no chance about it. It is part of the great onward movement of the world. It is human progress, but in this case it is a tremendous stride, a lifetime of ordinary momentum at a bound.

Century after century the waters of the "unsalted seas" leaped over Niagara's precipice, full of sound and fury, but signifying nothing beyond the grandeur of Nature in her wildest mood. Now, towards the close of the nineteenth century, this marvel of force is chained to man's uses, and a power sufficient to run the machinery of the world is levied upon for industrial purposes.

WHERE THE GOLDEN GRAIN IS STORED — THE ELEVATOR DISTRICT.

This tunnel project is a splendid illustration of human enterprise, of which there has been an endless procession of illustrations. Think of a few of the great things that have been accomplished. It became necessary to cross oceans, and sailing vessels were built. The application of steam came, and the ships folded their wings and flew faster than ever they did before. The world demanded swift speed upon land, and railroads were born, culminating in an Empire State Express that flies from New York to Buffalo in a little over eight hours. Lightning leaped from the clouds to copper wires and girdled the earth with instantaneous intelligence, and our voices speed swifter than thought from city to city.

The problems of the world are being solved one by one.

This is the electric age, and who can foretell what mighty things may come in the train of the pioneer work with Niagara's power! It is proposed at present to produce 125,000 horse-power. The *Scientific American* estimates that the force in Niagara's current amounts to several millions of horse-power. The present tunnel can be duplicated again and again as necessity demands. The sale of 15,000 horse-power will carry the present investment, leaving 110,000 horse-power for clear profit. The company has a capital of $10,000,000 to draw from, and a number of the greatest capitalists in the country are behind the movement. It is certain, then, that development will keep pace with the demand, and that all the electric power needed will be forthcoming. We have the great inexhaustible storehouse of Niagara to draw from forever, and human enterprise can be depended upon to dig the gold that may be had for the digging.

Buffalo, with her phenomenal facilities for tapping the mines, the lumber forests, the grain fields and all the other rich store-houses of the country, and with equal facilities for distributing the manufactured product, will, of course, be the chief market for the electric power produced at the Falls. It can be brought here without material loss in transmission, while the transportation advantages conferred by Buffalo's unique location cannot be transmitted. They are immovable as the eternal hills.

The result is not hard to trace. Buffalo is going to be the Electric City of the world, instead of the Queen City of the lakes.

In the larger manufacturing concerns here the cost of steam power has been brought down to about $35 per horse-power per year. The cost of power in the smaller manufacturing concerns is much greater than this sum.

It is estimated that the electric power from the Falls can be sold in Buffalo, ready for instant use by touching a button, at little more than half the present cost of steam power. Here is room for thought and comparison on the part of those engaged in manufacturing enterprises. Does not cheap power settle the question of a city's manufacturing greatness? Can there be any appeal from such settlement?

Give any city advantages in the way of cheap and abundant power not enjoyed by any other city on the face of the earth and what is the natural result? The eyes of manufacturers everywhere are focused upon that city.

Give to a city unequaled transportation facilities and the cheapest power in the world, and you have the conditions for building up the greatest industrial center in the world.

This is Buffalo's position.

Far-sighted men do not talk any more about the possibilities of Buffalo's future. They talk about certainties. They say with the New York *Tribune*: "The past of Buffalo is secure, and her manifest destiny is evidently to be something tremendous."

Truly, as has been said by Samuel Wilkeson, Buffalo holds the key to the commerce of an inland empire.

THE GROWTH OF A YEAR.

The Buffalo City Directory for 1892 shows about 6,000 more names than were contained in last year's directory. In order to compute the population of a city, it is usual to multiply the number of names in the directory by 3½, as, for the most part, only the names of heads of families appear there. Some cities multiply by 4. It is certainly very modest to make the multiplier 3¼, which is usually done in Buffalo. Upon this basis it will be seen that the increase in our population during the past year was 19,500, enough people gained in twelve months to make a city as large as Lockport, N. Y., and nearly as large as Oswego, N. Y. Counting 3¼ people to one name in the directory, we have a population, in June, 1892, of 297,375.

LAFAYETTE SQUARE AND SOLDIERS' MONUMENT

The increase during the year has been no more than the usual steady increase in the population of the city. With the addition of cheap electric power as a cause for growth, there can be no question but that the increase in future years will be much more rapid than in the past.

A GLOWING PROPHECY.

On February 19, 1888, before ever a drill had been started in the Niagara tunnel, and before the project had attracted much attention, the New York *Times* uttered this glowing prophecy for Buffalo:

"Every furrow turned on Dakota's plains, almost every blow struck with keen-edged axes in the forests that stand on the rugged Lake Superior region; the ceaseless hammering of compressed-air drills in Lake Vermillion iron mines; the work of thousands of Pennsylvania coal miners—in short, almost every blow struck in primary productive industry in the region tributary to the lakes adds to the prosperity of Buffalo … This region has proved to be the most productive of freight of all the lake regions, and the commerce of Lake Superior is still in its infancy … Buffalo will inevitably become the greatest milling city on earth."

THE GREAT SCIENTIFIC PAPER'S VIEW OF IT.

The *Scientific American*, in its issue of March 5, 1892, contained an extremely interesting article on the work and intentions of the Niagara Falls Power Company. After speaking of the methods of construction, etc., the article says:

"It is now the expectation of the company to make its first large contract for the delivery of power at a distance from the Falls, with the city of Buffalo, 3,000 horse-power being required for the lighting of the city. The present cost of a steam horse-power in Buffalo is put at $35 per year, and the company offers to contract to furnish power on its grounds at the Falls according to the following scale: For 5,000 horse-power, $10 per horse-power; for 4,500, $10.50; for 4,000, $11; and so on down to 300 horse-power, for which there will be charged $21 per horse-power per annum, each power to be supplied for twenty-four hour days. It is evident, therefore, that if the cost of transmission be within present expectations, the company will be able to furnish power at Buffalo at a much lower price than it is at present to be had at, and for a far larger field of usefulness than the mere lighting of the city. According to the most successful of all the recent efforts in the way of practically transmitting power electrically for a considerable distance, only about twenty-five per cent, of the power was lost in transmitting it by wire a distance of 108 miles. This degree of success was attained at the recent Frankfort exposition."

BUFFALO AND ITS ELECTRIC POWERHOUSE

WHAT ERASTUS WIMAN SAYS.

That well-known and successful financier, Erastus Wiman, of New York, who is deeply interested in electrical enterprises, read a very able paper at the convention of the National Electric Light Association held in Buffalo in February, 1892. In his paper he devoted considerable attention to the Niagara Falls tunnel scheme, and among other things he said;

"How vast is the internal commerce that throbs and pulsates over this fair land we may not now stop to estimate, and how important a part this great city of Buffalo is destined to play in it, electrically, we can only dimly guess. * * * The whole electrical community are watching with intense interest the possibility of the development in this city of Buffalo electrical transmission arising out of the successful effort which is now being made to harness the power hitherto latent in the Niagara River. The boldness of the proposal, the extent and character of the enterprise which is now nearing completion in this effort, the pluck and push in the work, challenge alike the attention of the engineering and the commercial world. The relation of this enormous power of nature to the transmission of electricity is the most important consideration which now occupies the thoughts of those most interested. The success which has attended the three-phase current from Lauffen to Frankfort in the transmission of power 112 miles, without material loss, comes just at the right moment to make it seem possible that the enormous potentialities in the forces of Niagara can be made to reach a degree of usefulness never dreamt of in the past and hardly realized in the wonderful present. It seems fortunate, therefore, that the convention which is here assembled should, as it were, be in the presence of the most stupendous event possible in the history of the science of electricity. In the development of the next few years will be found ample food for thought and effort, out of which may grow a relief for electric lighting plants of the greatest possible consequence. If in the city of Buffalo and from the Niagara River there can be transmitted power in such enormous proportions as are now contemplated, sub-divided and reduced, so that into every factory and almost into every house the force and energy can be controlled and operated, there is latent in every central station the possibilities that may come to every town in the country and to all electric light plants now lying idle during the day, an imitation in modified form of the power that of all forces in the world, Niagara is the best example."

"THE MANUFACTURING CENTRE OF THE NATION."

Within the past year or two, and particularly during 1892, Buffalo has received a great deal of attention from the press in all parts of the country. The leading newspapers of the large cities have discussed the question of Buffalo's future growth, and the general consensus of opinion has been that it will be phenomenally large.

Among the newspapers that have entered into this discussion is the Chicago *Tribune*. It stands in the front rank of the great journals of the United States. It is very ably edited, is a sterling, conservative newspaper, and its editorial utterances carry great weight. In its issue of March 13, 1892, it printed a leading editorial about Buffalo, and it is here produced in full:

"A recent article in the *Tribune* setting forth the prospect that this city will ere long be the centre of operations in the United States for the largest electrical company in the world has incited more than one good-humored protest that the people here are expecting too much. The New York *Tribune* and the Buffalo *Express* both call attention to the fact that Buffalo has great expectations in this matter of being the electrical centre of the world. With Niagara Falls behind it, and a consequence of the fact, Buffalo is claimed to be looming up as the chief manufacturing and shipping centre of the interior.

"In the course of a few months from now the practicability of converting the Falls into a source of power, light, heat, and refrigeration is to be demonstrated. A company is now constructing tunnels and setting a series of turbine wheels in position from which it is expected to obtain 120,000 horse-power without the combustion of a single pound of fuel. If it succeeds in this, every wheel in Buffalo can be turned and every building lighted and heated at the lowest possible cost. With this enormous electrical power transmitted to the city and distributed through it coal will no longer be burned there, and the steam engine will be dispensed within manufacturing processes. By virtue of having the cheapest power for turning its machinery Buffalo will inevitably become the manufacturing centre of the nation. This is the forecast made by practical electricians and endorsed by shrewd business men as a sound deduction, warranted, too, by a glance at the remarkable progress achieved by the city during the last decade.

"In that period the city at the foot of Lake Erie increased its coal traffic 387 per cent., its iron receipts 226 per cent., its population by 89 per cent., and fully doubled its grain receipts and lumber shipments. It is already the largest grain-receiving and coal-distributing center in the world, the principal lumber port in the country, and one of the greatest markets for live stock and fish. Its number of manufacturing establishments increased 200 per cent. from 1880 to 1890, and it is now considered certain that they will more than treble again by the end of the century with the conversion of the Falls into a source of electrical power, while the population will increase from 300,000 to 1,000,000. And it is said 'Buffalo now seems destined to gain steadily upon Chicago in the race for commercial supremacy.'

"That is a noble ambition, and the *Tribune* sees no reason to find fault with it. But it should not be forgotten that Chicago will also grow, so that Buffalo may still be a long way behind when her promise of a million inhabitants will have been realized. Yet it may be said that the prospects of growth are set forth only in a mild way by either of the papers named. If the transference of electrical power be performed as cheaply and efficiently as is now expected the result may be a speedy removal thither of much of the manufacturing industry of New England, a large share of the

'Yankee notion' business that now flourishes in those Eastern States, and no little of the manufacturing energy that at present exhibits itself in the smaller cities of New York and New Jersey. Possibly the silk industry of the latter will be found seeking the propinquity of the Falls. Troy and Rochester, particularly the latter, are likely to be injuriously affected, unless it be found that the power can be transmitted to them with but little loss, and Cleveland may be a great loser, while even the woolen mills of Philadelphia may be unable to compete with those of the new center. In short, the possibilities for paper mills, flour mills, cotton and woolen manufactories, and a host of other hives of industry clustering there is limited only by the quantity of power available from the descending waters, and this great prosperity will not bring with it the smudge of coal-burning, which has defiled the buildings and polluted the atmosphere of other cities that have attempted greatness by changing to more useful forms the raw products of nature. But it is hard to see how any or all of this can materially hurt Chicago, and the people of this city can well afford to wish those of Buffalo success in their new departure."

"ANOTHER MANCHESTER."

In a very able leading editorial, printed in the New York *Tribune* of February 7, 1892, the future of Buffalo was glowingly mirrored. Such utterances from such a source speak volumes, and show the commanding position to which Buffalo has risen — a position that attracts the attention of the newspapers of national eminence as well as of the greatest capitalists of the country. The article referred to is herewith printed entire:

"Chicago has been so intent upon rivaling New York in population and commercial importance that it has overlooked the chances of competition from another city in the Empire State. Buffalo, with Niagara Falls behind it, is looming up as the chief manufacturing and shipping center of the interior. In the coarse of a few months the practicability of converting the Falls into a source of power, light, heat and refrigeration is to be demonstrated. If the company which is now constructing tunnels and setting a series of turbine-wheels, succeeds in obtaining 120,000 horse-power, every wheel in Buffalo can be turned and every house lighted and heated at the lowest cost. With this enormous electrical power transmitted and distributed throughout the city, coal will no longer be burned and steam engines will be dispensed with in manufacturing processes. Buffalo, by virtue of having the cheapest power for turning its wheels, will inevitably become the manufacturing center of the nation. This is the forecast made, not only by sanguine electricians, but also by shrewd, practical business men, who have watched the remarkable progress of the city during the last decade.

"Even without the successful operation of the tunnel plant at Niagara, Buffalo since 1880 has increased its population 89 per cent., its grain receipts 101 per cent., its lumber shipments 125 per cent., its iron receipts 226 per cent., and its coal business

VIEW OF AN ASPHALTED STREET RESIDENCE.

387 per cent. The commerce of the great lakes has involved exchanges of wheat and coal. All the coal-carrying corporations have made Buffalo their shipping point for the West because the grain-laden fleet is available for return cargoes. The city is not only the largest grain-receiving and coal-distributing center in the world, but it is also the principal lumber port of the country and one of the greatest live-stock and fish markets. With coal, iron, lumber and salt available for the founding of new industries, it has increased its number of manufacturing industries over 200 per cent, during the last decade. These are substantial results which warrant the conclusion that the success of the project for converting Niagara Falls into a source of electric power will raise the population of Buffalo from 300,000 to 1,000,000 in another decade. The manufacturing interests of the country will inevitably center where electric power costing a fraction of either water or steam power can be supplied together with all raw materials. With the help of Niagara, Buffalo now seems destined to gain steadily upon Chicago in the race for commercial supremacy.

"It has been fortunate for Buffalo that prosperity has not overwhelmed it suddenly, and that it has had leisure for preparing for its good fortune. Already it is the handsomest residence city in America, with broad, heavily-shaded streets paved with asphalt, with a well-designed series of beautiful parks, and with public buildings, hotels, libraries and music halls worthy of a great town. If its wealthy class live in luxurious palaces incomparably finer than the residences of Eastern millionaires, its poor and humble artisans are housed in neat and tasteful cottages. It is a charming city of homes and domestic comfort, which is gradually being transformed into one of the busiest hives of American manufacturing industry. It is at least a pleasant thought that through the transmission of power now going to waste at Niagara this well-kept and wholesome town may escape the smudge of coal-burning which has fouled Chicago and impaired the freshness and beauty of Cleveland. If by the end of another decade every wheel in it from the trolleys on the electric railways to the largest iron lathe in its engineering works be turned by power generated by the turbines at Niagara, it will be another Manchester, but without smoke and grime."

AMERICA'S HANDSOMEST CITY.

The latter portion of the *Tribune* article draws attention to some very noteworthy facts connected with Buffalo. When the *Tribune* says that Buffalo is "the handsomest residence city in America," it tells the exact truth. All Buffalonians are deservedly proud of the beauties of their city. Many times has the writer heard exclamations of surprise and delight from the lips of strangers who, for the first time, were being driven through our beautiful avenues and park roads. Our streets are exceptionally wide and well-paved. Care in tree-planting has led to magnificent results. Well-kept, velvety lawns of spacious extent are the rule, and make fine setting for the thousands of architectural gems of homes with which the city is studded. It has been said over and over again by

FAR-FAMED DELAWARE AVENUE.

traveled strangers that Buffalo has more fine architecture in residences, more beautiful homes than any other city of its size in the world. We had, at the close of the summer of 1891, about 105 lineal miles of asphalted streets. It is hard as a rock and smooth as a floor and full of restful delight to those who drive over its smooth, clean surface. Personal pride taken by the property-owners in its trim beauty leads to its being swept and cleaned daily, which is done at trifling expense. Asphalt is being laid in this city at the rate of about twenty lineal miles per year, and we have now more miles of asphalted streets than any other city in the world.

The park system of Buffalo contains about 900 acres of handsome land, which has been laid out by Frederick L. Olmsted, the eminent landscape artist, and its natural beauty wonderfully added to. It lies close to the finer residence portion of the city, and is readily reached from all sections. Land for new parks on the south side of the city and along the lake has recently been bought, making splendid additions to the park system.

The school system of Buffalo ranks deservedly high. We have over fifty grammar schools, one high school, another large school building used for the overflow and a new high school projected. We have a State Normal School, Kindergartens, dozens of parochial and private schools, and we have taken steps to establish manual training schools.

We have medical colleges of high standing, business colleges of national reputation, some splendid public libraries, several of the finest theaters in the country, and handsome churches without number. No city has more right than has Buffalo to be called the city of churches. We have about 150 of them.

The social atmosphere of Buffalo is delightful, and visitors to this city always carry away with them very pleasant memories of our social life.

In short, there is in Buffalo every refinement of civilization of the highest type. The busy man of affairs who seeks, at the same time, investment for his capital and charming social advantages for his family, can find in Buffalo all that he desires.

A CITY OF HOMES.

And there is still another phase of this subject that should be touched upon. Buffalo is a city of homes for the humble as well as the rich. It is a city full of the sweet content that belongs to the home-builder. Building and loan associations, of which we have a great number, have materially helped to bring about this result. But it is a fact that these associations thrive only in soil suited to them. They are the outgrowth of sterling worth, sobriety and manly ambition. Where they thrive we find good workmen of conservative instincts, who are averse to taking part in labor troubles. This is believed to be the chief reason why Buffalo has always enjoyed a singular freedom from strikes. Be the cause what it may, it is a fact that strikes are of a rare occurrence here; and when they have occurred they have been quickly settled. The firebrands of labor agitations have had very little encouragement here.

It is the more easy for workmen to own their own homes in Buffalo from the fact that land values here are remarkably low. We stretch over a large section of territory and have plenty of room for our people.

A first-class electric street car service gives easy and swift access to the suburbs; while the New York Central Railroad runs trains every hour each way on a Belt Line encircling the city and tapping residence portions all around the fifteen-mile circuit.

Nowhere is there a more conservative, prosperous and contented community of workingmen than in Buffalo, and this is a fact that builds up a bulwark of safety for industrial enterprises and investment of capital.

OUR ELECTRIC RAILROAD SYSTEM.

Rapid transit is one of the essentials in the busy life of a great city. Buffalo has outgrown the horse car system and has now swift electric cars speeding in all directions. All the great arteries of travel leading from the heart of the city are equipped with electric cars. The work of putting in the electric system has been one of great magnitude, as there was no cessation in the traffic while the change was being made.

Though electric cars have been in operation in some of the park roads for several years, the work of changing the system in down town streets was not started until the fall of 1890. Work was then begun on Niagara Street, and on July 4, 1891, the first electric cars were run in that important thoroughfare. Within four months traffic on the line was tripled, and it has steadily increased ever since. Elk, Seneca, Washington and Sycamore streets, all thoroughfares leading to the suburbs, were next equipped with electric cars, and at this writing (June, 1892) the work of changing the system in Main Street is progressing rapidly, and is almost completed. The system is, of course, being changed in the most important thoroughfares first, and the less important lines will undergo the same treatment in rapid succession, so that it will not be very long before horse cars will be remembered in Buffalo as the vanished symbol of a slower era. The total length of the street railroad tracks of Buffalo is over 100 miles.

Through the chief thoroughfares the electric cars run every three minutes. A single fare of five cents is charged from one end of the city to the other, with the privilege of changing from one line to another. There are no transfer charges. The company pays to the city a percentage on its earnings of two to three per cent., graded in proportion to the amount of the gross receipts. This arrangement, which was entered into during the early part of 1892, was a very welcome one to the people, particularly to workingmen, who consequently are enabled to reach their work in any part of the city, even the most distant, for a five cent fare. The swiftness of the electric cars, from eight to eighteen miles an hour, is a great factor in time-saving, and it is much appreciated by working people, as well as by business men, and all who are impatient of delay in getting from one part of the city to another.

The Buffalo Railway Company, which operates all the lines of street railroad in the city, has a capital of six million dollars, so that it is financially strong and able to carry out any improvement desired.

Cheap electric power from Niagara will, of course, be available in the running of street cars in Buffalo; and as it can be bought very much cheaper than it can be produced by the evaporation of steam it will have a potent influence in making it possible for the company to grant still further concessions to the public. The citizens' committee which recently arbitrated between the company and the public and brought about the present satisfactory agreement had full and free access to all the books of the company, and figured out to a nicety the cost of carrying each passenger, and the amount of profit in the business. If the cost of the motive power had been cut in two, as it will be cut by the introduction of Niagara's power, the committee would certainly have reported in favor of even better terms for the city. Thus it is a fair conclusion that the beneficent effects of cheap power generated at the Falls will be felt by every person who rides on the street cars of Buffalo.

This subject is here dwelt upon at considerable length because the writer feels that it is of great importance. Every manufacturer whose eyes are turned in this direction, and who is considering whether he shall take advantage of the peerless opportunities now offered in Buffalo, wants to know about the street car service. He wants to know, in case he should locate his plant here, how quickly and how cheaply he and his employees could get to and from their business. It is a pleasure to assure him and all others interested that the electric street railroad system of Buffalo is pronounced by experts to be the best in the United States, and also that its management is of the most liberal and progressive kind.

The street car service of a city is part of its throbbing life, part of its pulse, and by it the business health and prosperity of the city can be gauged.

SUBURBAN ELECTRIC ROADS.

Within a radius of a few miles from Buffalo there are many thriving towns. Naturally, with so many steam railroads running in all directions from this point, residents of these towns enjoy excellent railroad accommodations in traveling to and from the city. But the swift pace of present progress is all too rapid for the old way. Electric lines to suburban towns are being built or projected in surprising number. An electric line to the city of Tonawanda, connecting with the Buffalo street railroad system, and in fact being an extension of it, has been in successful operation since early in the present year (1892). It will be extended through to Niagara Falls. Two other lines of electric railroad to Tonawanda have been surveyed and active preparations are being made to build them. Both will connect with the Buffalo system, and in time will be extended to Niagara Falls. One of these has secured a very favorable route, out

Delaware Avenue in a direct air line to Tonawanda, through a delightful residence district.

An electric railroad is being built to Lancaster and Depew, the latter being the new city of the New York Central Railroad just outside of Buffalo, where the Central's locomotive shops, the Gould Car Coupler Works and other great industrial enterprises are in progress. This line will be in operation by September of this year.

Still another electric line is to be built to East Aurora, the prettiest of Erie County villages, where the famous Hamlin and Jewett stock farms are located. C. J. Hamlin, the millionaire horseman, and owner of Belle Hamlin, is one of the prominent men interested in this line.

Strong companies have also been formed to build electric lines to Hamburg, Williamsville and other suburban towns.

All of these enterprises indicate the profound belief which capitalists have in Buffalo's future. Most of them were brought into life through the stimulating influence of cheap electric power from Niagara Falls. Those interested in these enterprises knew that cheap electric power meant tremendous and rapid growth for the city, and that the tide of prosperity would sweep out far enough to reach all towns lying contiguous to the city, and whose prosperity is part of the prosperity of Buffalo. They also knew that cheap electric power from Niagara Falls meant cheap motive power for their roads and greatly reduced cost of operation.

It is a modest assertion that the silent, swift, all-powerful currents of electricity flowing into Buffalo from Niagara will touch every craft, every branch of industry. It will quicken all these into renewed activity and point a thousand new ways for the employment of money, brains and muscle. It will give us light, heat and refrigeration, and power for the mightiest and most delicate machinery.

The smoke cloud of industry that hovers over and shrouds the manufacturing district of every great city, will gradually lift from ours as the consumption of coal gives place to smokeless electric power. In a few years it will be all gone, and Buffalo, the "Electric City," will be famed as the cleanest and healthiest city in the world.

THE BUFFALO LIBRARY.

"BUFFALO'S GOLD MINE."

Some years ago, Mr. James B. Stafford, of this city, then president of the Buffalo Business Men's Association, conceived the idea of offering a prize of $100,000 for the best plan of utilizing the current of Niagara River. He and over one hundred others subscribed $1,000 each to a fund for the purpose, and the attention of scientific men in all parts of the civilized world was directed to the problem. This problem has been solved in the development of the tunnel project.

Mr. Stafford is a keen, shrewd, level-headed business man, and has made a large fortune by judicious investments in Buffalo real estate. He believes that Buffalo will have a million population within ten years, as a result of an industrial revolution in this city that will amaze the world, the chief and controlling reason for which will be the introduction of cheap electric power.

In the Buffalo *Commercial* of December 22, 1891, the following interview with Mr. Stafford was printed, under the heading "Buffalo's Gold Mine:"

"If the richest gold mine in the whole world were discovered in a suburb of Buffalo, what effect do you suppose it would have on our people?" asked Mr. James B. Stafford of a *Commercial* reporter.

"There would be tremendous excitement, of course," was the reply.

"There would," returned Mr. Stafford; "but do you know that the richest gold mine in the world would be a mere bagatelle compared with the wealth that will spring from the Niagara Falls tunnel? Do our people stop to think what it means? It means prosperity for Buffalo beyond the wildest present expectation. I believe I speak entirely within bounds when I say that it will make Buffalo the second greatest city in the whole United States, and that you and I won't be very old when our city reaches that place. Looking into the immediate future, I will prophesy that we will have a million population within ten years.

"Just look about you and see what electricity has already done for the world, and yet we are scarcely entered upon the Electric Age. We are at the dawn of a new era, and electricity, now in its infancy, will grow and develop until it revolutionizes the world. It will give us power, light, heat, refrigeration. It will do everything for us that steam now does, and here in Buffalo it is going to cost less than water power."

"What does it cost manufacturers for power now?"

"The water power of the country now in use costs from $16.67 per horse-power per year at Lockport to $56.25 at Manayunk, Pa., while steam costs all the way from $35 to $175 per horse-power per annum.

"When we consider that the entire power going to waste at the Falls is one-seventh of the entire power of the world one can comprehend what an inexhaustible mine of wealth we are on the eve of developing. Already the problem of transmitting electricity long distances without much waste has been solved. Other companies are in the field, and before many years instead of 125,000 horse power there will probably be a million. Buffalo being the nearest large city to the great cataract, it will be the first to receive the benefits.

"Just let your mind run forward a dozen years. Electricity running through cables from the Falls will act on our city like the warm blood running through a human body, will permeate every part of the city, running 2,000 horse-power engines as easily as the dentist's drill or the family sewing machine. Every wheel in Buffalo will be eventually turned by electricity. It will light and heat our houses. It will be cheaper than anything else. The impetus that it will give our manufacturing enterprises will be incalculable.

"Add to all this our great natural advantages and no wonder our expectations should be great. We are midway between the great producing regions of the West and the more thickly populated sections of the East, with its continually increasing export trade. What better point could be found for the manufacturing centre of the country? Here all the shipping from the western chain of lakes discharges its cargoes of grain, lumber, ore, etc., reloading with up-cargoes of coal (and all the great coal-carrying transportation corporations have branches that now terminate in this city), laying at the door of the manufacturer the raw material at the lowest possible freight rate, with twenty-six lines of railroads leading from here in every direction (many of them trunk lines), with a canal and waterway to the seaboard giving the manufacturer the finest shipping facilities possible.

"Buffalo already boasts of the largest coal distributing point in the world, the largest sheep and fresh fish market in the world; one of the largest horse markets; the largest grain distributing point in the world; the second largest cattle market in the world; we are destined to be the largest flour milling city in the world, and with our suburban port of Tonawanda we have the largest lumber market in the world.

"In the last ten years we have increased our population 89 per cent., and with this new and wonderful factor that no other city in the world's history has ever had, it is not a wild statement to make, but one that the present outlook would warrant, that Buffalo and not Chicago will be the second American city."

ELECTRIC POWER ON THE CANADIAN SIDE.

Col. Albert D. Shaw, formerly U. S. Consul at Montreal, Canada, and later at Manchester, England, is at the head of a company which proposes to produce electricity on the Canadian side of the Niagara River. This company has secured the passage of a bill through the Ontario Parliament permitting the incorporation of a company with a capitalization of $3,000,000, and a privilege of bonding to the extent of $5,000,000, with the object of producing electricity by means of a tunnel upon the Canadian side.

In conversation with a writer for the Philadelphia *Press*, in April of this year, Col. Shaw said the Canadian company had not been organized to compete with the American company, but rather to supplement and act in concert with it. He explained that as the land on the Canadian side is devoted to park purposes, it cannot be used for the location of manufactories, and therefore the power produced must be transmitted to other points. In this connection he went on to say:

"Such power can certainly be carried to Buffalo. An electrical plant has been established about 16 miles from the city of Rome, N. Y., and the power there furnished is conveyed to Rome with perfectly satisfactory results. Buffalo is only a little more than 20 miles from Niagara, and with the higher voltage which can be obtained there is no doubt that city can be furnished with electric power sufficient to run all the manufactories of New York State were they located there. After our company is organized in harmony with the New York company we shall begin work, and I think can complete it within a year."

"The water power furnished by the Niagara River above the Falls," continued Col. Shaw, "is estimated to be equivalent to 3,000,000 horse-power. When we recollect that the Connecticut River at Holyoke only furnishes about 24,000 horse-power, and the river at Minneapolis only 18,000, some idea can be obtained of this enormous power which has hitherto been going to waste. The American company has built a tunnel 8,000 feet long. The entrance to it is a long distance above the Falls, and the exit where the waste water flows into the Niagara River is just below the suspension bridge. This tunnel is capable of furnishing power equivalent to 140,000 horse-power, an amount of power which vastly exceeds anything furnished anywhere else in the world. The Niagara River never runs dry. There never is an appreciable diminution in its body of water. Everywhere else where water power is used manufactories are compelled either to have a steam plant which can be relied upon in dry weather, or else to run the risk of shutting down for lack of power. That can never happen on the banks of the Niagara."

Col. Shaw went on to speak of the plans of the American company, with which he is familiar. After stating that manufacturers from all parts of the country have been in communication with the American company with a view of locating plants in the city of Buffalo, and that expert engineers estimate that the electric power which can be developed and furnished will be practically illimitable, he said:

"The Canadian company will be able to furnish tremendous voltage whenever wires properly insulated are ready to receive it. The New York capitalists who virtually own the American company, and will be in harmony with the Canadian, are even more enthusiastic than they are in Buffalo. I have talked with a number of them since I have been in the city. They are careful men, not likely to be carried away with false enthusiasm, and who look at such things purely from a commercial point of view.

NATURE AT HER LOVELIEST   THE PARK LAKE.

They are of opinion, as I am, and as everybody else is who has made a study of this matter, that the great manufacturing city of the future is to be located upon the bank of the Niagara River, and the time is not far distant when the city of Buffalo will extend from its present site full twenty miles to the north. The number of manufactories which have already decided to move from various other towns, some of them in the far West, to Buffalo, is an indication of what the future will be.

"The power is permanent and is dependent upon no changes of the weather. Moreover, it is cheap power, and will always be sufficient, no matter how greatly any manufacturer may desire to increase his plant. Furthermore, the contiguity of this place to convenient transportation is another temptation to manufacturers. For instance, it has been demonstrated that the grain of the West can be brought there and manufactured into flour at least 10 cents a barrel cheaper than in the great milling cities of the West, and that of itself is a handsome profit.

"Furthermore, transportation charges, such is the relation of Buffalo and its vicinity to water and rail routes, will be cheaper there than at any other manufacturing center in the United States. The raw material can be brought either by the lakes or by rail to the doors of the mill, and the finished product can be sent out by lake, by the Canadian Canal to the St. Lawrence River, by the Erie Canal during the season when water transportation is open, and there are 26 different lines of railway centering there. The manufacturers have been figuring pretty closely. Competition is so great that it is frequently the economies which represent the difference between success and failure, profit and loss. All those of them who have already decided to locate in that vicinity and utilize this great power are of opinion that the saving in expenses will of itself represent a fair profit on the capital invested. Within 20 years it would not be surprising to see a city, or a link of cities practically one, containing 1,000,000 people, and perhaps the largest capital investment in manufacturing in the United States, with perhaps one or two exceptions.

"It is strange that this magnificent power which has been wasted heretofore should not have had earlier development. Several attempts have been made to develop it, but capital has been timid until some of the great financial geniuses of New York City became interested."

ELECTRICITY IN THE HOUSEHOLD.

It is certain that electricity will be so cheap and plentiful in Buffalo that it will come into general use in the homes of our people. It will be cheaper than gas for light, and coal for heat. It will run the family sewing machine. The electric motor will become a part of every well-ordered household. The *Scientific American*, speaking of the new uses of electricity coming in the train of its cheap production, says:

"Domestic life will be attended with many comforts and conveniences. The cook will only need to touch a button, and presto, her electrical stove will be in full operation, the pot will boil, the oven bake, the turkey roast, the pump move, the washing

WATERWORKS POWER HOUSE AND INLET PIER IN NIAGARA RIVER.

machine turn; while the electric refrigerator will freeze the water, preserve the meats, vegetables, milk, butter, eggs, and other supplies. No coal, no wood, no dust, no dirt, no oil, no gas. The lady of the house will be relieved of care. She presses a button, and every nook and corner of her dwelling glows with cheerful light. Touch another and the electric fire glimmers in every room, diffusing genial warmth. The electric lift takes her up or down stairs. The telephone conveys her orders to market, and distributes her social commands among friends and neighbors."

ELECTRICITY'S MANIFOLD USES.

In the same article occurs a concise statement of the varied uses to which the incoming low-priced power will be applied in Buffalo. It is as follows:

"Near to Niagara, only twenty-two miles distant, is Buffalo, already a large and prosperous city, the head centre of lake navigation. The simple extension of conductors over the short distance above mentioned will bring to the people of Buffalo direct share in the economic and other advantages of the new and great enterprise. Light, heat and motive power for streets, vehicles works, shops, factories, stores, churches, dwellings, can be supplied from the dynamos at Niagara more economically, probably, than by any other means. Local steam engines may be dismissed; their occupation, for Buffalo, will be gone. Even the steam fire engines may retire. The electric pump will beat them out of sight."

PLENTY OF BANKING CAPITAL.

Buffalo is blessed with splendid banking facilities. There are now nineteen banks of deposit in the city with a total capital of nearly five million dollars and a reserve of nearly eleven millions. Five new banks have been started here since the spring of 1891. Our bankers are cautious, conservative business men, and banking business in this city has always been conducted on conservative lines. The solid financiers who control these great barometers of our business life have never invited disaster by loose, speculative methods. Like the arch in the foundation wall of a massive structure, gaining strength from increased weight, has been the prudence of our bankers, and to-day our banking institutions rest upon secure foundation and are ready for the branching out and growth that will come to them with the rapid increase in industrial enterprises resulting from the world's cheapest power. Prudence has been the watchword of success in the past, and it will continue as the governor in the greater transactions of the greater future.

OUR LOW TAX RATE.

Some facts about Buffalo's tax rate are fitting at this time. In a carefully written article from the pen of the Hon. Charles F. Bishop, Mayor of Buffalo, and printed in the Sunday *Express* of April 3, 1892, the following facts are given:

"Property in Buffalo is assessed at much less than its real value, and its tax rate has for many years, for all purposes (State, County and City) except local improvements, averaged about two dollars per hundred on the assessment. At first thought this may seem high, but a careful examination of the reports of other cities shows that the rate elsewhere is generally much higher. In New York it is $1.95; in Chicago $5.00; in Brooklyn $2.57; in Cleveland it is $2.79; in Cincinnati $2.85. And this reasonable rate of taxation is not obtained by rapid increase of our bonded indebtedness except for acquiring valuable property for permanent use, or the extension of great public improvements.

"Indeed, so careful has the increase of indebtedness been guarded that now with an indebtedness of $11,464,531 the city is the owner of real estate valued, in 1890, at $7,804,267 and personal property valued at $6,828,765. . Surely this statement shows a due regard for the tax-payers' interests; and coupled with the fact that Buffalo maintains school facilities as good as those of any city, police and fire departments that for efficiency are unsurpassed, and furnishes a water supply that for purity and cheapness is unequaled, it presents a very well-grounded claim for municipal economy.

"The total of assessments annually shows a gratifying increase of wealth, and of necessity the expenses of the city must also increase with greater population to serve and more extended public improvements to maintain. I am sanguine, however, that in a few years the increase in values will create a noticeable decrease of tax rate."

OUR CITY WATER.

Buffalo's source of water supply is the same as the source of our marvelous electric power. It is the Niagara. We get it pure and undefiled, in unlimited quantity, and it is as cheap as it is pure and plentiful. The service is under the control of the city government. Our water rates are cheaper than those in any other large city in the country, manufacturers are given very low special rates, and yet there are several hundred thousand dollars available every year for further extensions to keep pace with the rapid growth of the city, which is constantly pushing out and developing in new sections. The pumping engines and entire plant are first-class in every particular.

Niagara's water, as is generally known, comes down from the great lakes, and enters the river at the foot of Lake Erie, where Buffalo is located. A mile down stream is an inlet pier through which the water supply for the city is drawn by mammoth pumping engines. Analysis shows that there is no organic matter in the water, and that it is absolutely pure. There is an entire absence of any possibility of its being defiled before it reaches Buffalo. All dredgings from the Buffalo harbor and river, canal and slips must be and are, as provided by stringent law, dumped below the inlet pier.

Thus it will be seen that this great requisite in the health and prosperity of a city is assured in pure and unlimited supply forever.

NATURAL GAS FUEL.

A very large section of the residence portion of Buffalo is supplied with natural gas fuel. It is brought in pipes from Pennsylvania, and also from Canada, and is extensively used for fuel in this city. It is sold to consumers for 25 cents per thousand feet net, and on an average costs no more than coal. The freedom which it gives from the task of handling coal and ashes, and the entire absence of dust and dirt in connection with its use, are greatly appreciated in thousands of Buffalo homes. The Canadian supply gives rich promise of abundant yield, and its principal market is in Buffalo. The source of the Canadian supply is only a few miles from Buffalo. The tremendous extent of the Pennsylvania field is well known.

ELECTRICITY SUPPLANTING STEAM.

As electric power has heretofore been produced, for the most part, by the consumption of coal and evaporation of steam, it has had to compete with steam on disadvantageous terms, as the steam lay one step nearer the base of the power, namely, the fuel.

Coal produced steam; steam, in turn, produced electricity; and as success in any line of manufacture consists largely in the application of economical methods, steam power has been preferred to electric power because it has been cheaper, except, probably, in running small plants with electricity supplied from a central station. In Rochester, N. Y., this is done to a very considerable extent, the idea being that electricity produced by steam can be furnished from a central station to many small factories as cheaply or almost as cheaply as steam power could be produced on a small scale in each one of the factories. The centralization of the power economizes both in machinery and labor. In larger plants, however, it has been found impossible to produce electricity from steam power to compete with steam. Waste in the process, steam being the parent force, prevents a pound of coal from producing as much electric power as steam power. To accomplish such a thing would be like turning base metal into gold.

But with electric power produced by the water power of the Niagara Falls tunnel, steam is dethroned as the King of Force. Electricity takes its place and builds an empire on the banks of the Niagara. And the heart of that empire is Buffalo, and will be forever. The wonderful power has its source near to us; only a few miles of copper wire brings it to our workshops; and here are concentrated shipping facilities unequaled upon the continent. Economy in collecting the raw material, and distributing it again in the shape of manufactured articles, is as important as economy in manufacturing. With cheap power from the Niagara we have the two great economies joined. What a tremendous aggregation of advantages! No wonder conservative business men prophesy a million population for Buffalo within ten years. No wonder the New York *Tribune* says that our "manifest destiny is evidently to be something tremendous."

ROOM IN WHICH TO GROW.

When a person undertakes to point out sections of Buffalo that will be most affected by cheap electric power he is confronted with a difficult task. It is certain that the entire manufacturing district will at once respond to the vivifying influence of the electric currents, and that new industrial sections will be opened up at many points. Manufactories will be enlarged, hundreds of new ones will be started, as hundreds of manufacturers from the outside will crowd in to take advantage of the splendid opportunities open to all. Fortunately, we have a great deal of room in which factories may grow and spread, and as the railroads tap a very large portion of the city, there need be no fear of restricted shipping facilities. Although Buffalo has a population of nearly 300,000, its population per acre is only 10.23. St. Louis is 11.51; Cleveland, 16.41; Cincinnati, 18.56; San Francisco, 30.22; Brooklyn, 47.62; New York, 58.87.

These figures are full of suggestion. There is room in Buffalo. And beyond the city line there are thousands of broad acres ready to be used for factories or homes.

There has been a steady, legitimate increase in values in all parts of the city and surrounding country. Particularly in the northern part of the city, to the north of the park, among lands lying in the direction from which the electric currents will flow, there has been a strong movement, and it is probably true that this foreshadows a growth in values that will be startling to many.

Far-seeing men forecast the future by picturing a city that will grow towards the seat of the electric current, followed always by the railroads in the path of progress, until Tonawanda is reached and absorbed; and stretching further still, will finally reach the great cataract itself. Is this too much to expect of a city that holds within its exclusive grasp the two great economies — cheap power, cheap freights! It is well to keep these two things steadily in mind.

But as the city grows in length it will grow in breadth. It will widen out on all sides, and all parts of the city will share in the general prosperity.

THE PHILADELPHIA & READING.

Nothing gives better evidence of the growing importance of Buffalo than recent action of the Philadelphia & Reading Railroad Company. This great company has at Philadelphia and along the Delaware River greater terminal facilities than any other railroad company operating on the Atlantic seaboard. In February, 1892, it obtained control of the Lehigh Valley system, thereby securing a direct route from Buffalo to Philadelphia. The new and more active management saw the tremendous importance of obtaining a foothold in Buffalo, which already holds the key to the traffic of the great lakes, and now stands upon the verge of extraordinary manufacturing development by reason of Niagara's cheap and unlimited power. Within a comparatively few years Buffalo will be the chief manufacturing center of the country; the possibilities of traffic radiating from this point are boundless. It was a master stroke of President McLeod of the Philadelphia & Reading to establish his railroad securely in Buffalo. It is a well-known fact that the Lehigh Valley has the

THE ERIE COUNTY SAVINGS BANK — A MILLION DOLLAR BUILDING.

best terminal facilities of all the railroads centering here. Within the past few years millions have been spent in perfecting them.

Following this stroke with the Lehigh Valley, the Philadelphia & Reading made a traffic contract with the Buffalo, Rochester & Pittsburg for fifty years, giving still further evidence of belief in Buffalo.

The export business of the Philadelphia & Reading is vast, operating as it does in connection with a line of transatlantic steamers, and this opens up a new line of thought. The impetus given by cheap and plentiful power to manufacturing in old and many new directions in Buffalo will of course be very great, and it is certain that thousands of industries depending upon export trade will flourish here, close to the storehouses of the raw material and of the world's cheapest power. Numerous avenues to the seaboard are therefore an essential part of the grand plan of our industrial prosperity, and the addition of the Philadelphia & Reading is one of very great importance.

Yet this should always be held in mind — would the Philadelphia & Reading have reached out after Buffalo business if it had not been worth while reaching for? The fact is that we attract great transportation enterprises as the magnet does the needle.

THE UNION IRON WORKS.

During the present summer the Union Iron Works, long unused, are being rebuilt in the southern part of the city, the plans calling for one of the finest plants of the kind in the United States. Part of the plant will be used for the manufacture of steel, and at the beginning a force of about 1,200 men will be employed in this part of the works alone, in three shifts of eight hours each, work being constant night and day all the year 'round.

What stimulus is it that brings this industry into life? Why was it not located at any one of a dozen other points that might be named? Why wasn't it located close to the iron mines? These and all other collateral questions have already been answered in this volume. We have power cheaper than the cheapest anywhere else, joined with transportation facilities that are unexcelled — the two great industrial economies again, cheap power, cheap freights.

THE COPPER INDUSTRY.

One of the largest aggregations of capital in the world is the Calumet & Hecla Smelting Company. It controls the rich copper mines of Lake Superior with all their inexhaustible stores of wealth. Two years ago the company bought a very large tract of land on the banks of the Niagara within the city limits of Buffalo, and began the construction of an extensive smelting works. The ore is brought here direct from the mines, and here it is reduced and the whole output of the mines distributed from this point. Why did the Calumet & Hecla Company locate in Buffalo? Because of its peerless location as a distributing centre for one thing, and cheap electric power for another.

Not long ago, in Buffalo, a live electric wire fell athwart a lamp post, and in the twinkling of an eye the iron was fused by the current. That was smelting by electricity. The brainy men of the Calumet & Hecla Company knew what they were doing when they located beside Buffalo's electric power house.

ENORMOUS MANUFACTURING CAPITAL.

The foregoing are simply instances of many new enterprises that have lately been started in Buffalo. The manufacturing establishments of this city tripled during the ten years between 1880 and 1890, and the proportion of increase since 1890 has been much greater than before. It is believed that the capital invested in manufacturing enterprises of all kinds in Buffalo amounts to nearly $100,000,000. What will it be after the full force of Niagara's lightning has struck us?

AN ETERNAL POWER HOUSE.

The source of Buffalo's electrical power is the force in running water, but unlike almost every other water power it is never-ceasing. Its supply comes from the hills and watersheds of half a continent. The Niagara can never run dry, can never diminish in volume to make an iota of difference. It is the narrow end of a funnel through which a resistless force must ever flow. It is a force that will always exist. For all time the power of the Niagara developed into electricity will turn the wheels of industry within the great city upon its banks. No emergency steam plants will be needed, as on the banks of many rivers, to supply the place of failing water power. Niagara's power is eternal.

A GREAT FIELD FOR INVESTORS.

Nowhere on the North American continent is there so grand a field for investment as in Buffalo. Values here have been and are phenomenally low. It has been and is a conservative city. There has never been a boom in Buffalo. There has been increase in values, but no inflation, no boom. Talk of a Buffalo boom has been heard, but the presence of a boom is here denied most emphatically and earnestly. Values in Buffalo and vicinity are lower than in any other progressive city of its size in the country. There has been so much available land that inflation has been checked. A great deal of Buffalo property has changed hands within the past year or two, but at very reasonable figures. Millions will be made within a few years by landholders, and without effort on their part. A dollar planted in the soil of Buffalo today will spring up as two dollars next year.

When a city doubles its population it at the same time quadruples the value of its real estate. It is freely prophesied that Buffalo's population will be doubled in five years, quadrupled in ten. The cheapest power in the world and unequalled shipping facilities — by railroad, lake and canal — will produce this wonderful metamorphosis.

Cheap power! Cheap freights! A world of wealth is contained in the combination.

Buffalo has a most substantial foundation on which to build a manufacturing metropolis. It is a conservative city, full of careful, cautious business men. It has come along by comparatively slow and always steady progress, taking no forward step until strong and ready for it. Commercial depressions have affected us but little. Panics have avoided us, for panics are like plagues and seize hold where the conditions are unhealthy. We have had neither plagues nor panics; we have a healthy city physically and financially.

Now a new era has dawned. We are about to leap to an eminence undreamed of in years gone by. Strong from the strength of right business living we are equal to the swifter pace of the new order of things. The sublime force of the Niagara is chained and diverted to manufacturing uses. Every wheel in Buffalo will be turned by this marvelous power at far less cost than machinery can be run anywhere else in the wide world. There's a giant force behind the leap. Cheap power! Cheap freights! These are the talismanic symbols of a mighty greatness.

GREAT IMPORTANCE OF THE LAKE TRAFFIC.

The *Review of Reviews*, in a recent article on the traffic of the Great Lakes, proves the extraordinary importance of this traffic and of Buffalo's location from a commercial standpoint. It must always be borne in mind that the great bulk of the lake traffic is tributary to Buffalo. The article referred to is as follows:

> "Few persons who have not made a personal study of the matter realize the magnitude of the traffic of the Great Lakes. There were over 1,100 more vessels passing through the canal into Duluth, Minnesota, in 1891, than passed through the Suez Canal the year previous. Through the 'Soo' Canal at the outlet of Lake Superior there were more than three times as many vessels and nearly a million and three-quarters tons more freight in 1890 than through the Suez Canal during the same year. There is not the same absolute record of vessels passing through the Detroit River as is obtainable for the two points previously mentioned. But an estimate made by Hon. George H. Ely, of Cleveland, shows that in 1889 there were more than 36,000,000 tons of freight carried through the Detroit River. This sum seems large when it is stated by itself, but the real magnitude will perhaps be better appreciated when it is known that this is 10,000,000 tons in excess of the tonnage at all the seaports of the United States for the same year, and 3,000,000 tons in excess of the total arrivals and clearances, both coastwise and foreign, of Liverpool and London combined. The arrivals and clearances of vessels at Chicago for 1890 numbered 21,541, while the corresponding aggregate for New York was but 15,283. The entries and clearances for the entire seaboard of the United States in that year were 37,756, while for the United States ports on the Great Lakes the arrivals and clearances numbered 88,280. The traffic of the Great Lakes in 1891 was 27 per cent of the total traffic of all the railways of the United States for the same year, and if the tonnage carried on the lakes had been carried instead by rail, at the average price per ton per mile, it would have cost, in round numbers, $150,000,000 more than was actually paid for its transportation by water."

BEAUTIFUL GRAND ISLAND.

Down the Niagara river from Buffalo a few miles the noble stream divides and forms Grand Island. This is Buffalo's watering-place. Hotels, club-houses, summer residences and public pleasure grounds abound all along the river's banks on either side of the island, while the rich farming land of the interior is devoted to agriculture. The air of the island is pure, the scenery delightful, and the ride upon the river to and from the city is full of restful charm.

Many pleasure steamers ply between the city and the island resorts, and do a large and remunerative business. But for the great mass of busy people some sort of transit more rapid than steamers is necessary. This want is about to be met. A project has lately ripened to build a bridge from the mainland and run an electric railroad across the bridge and clear around the island, connecting with the street railroad system of the city. Long-headed men foresee that when this is accomplished there will be a quick and large appreciation of land values on the island, and it is certain that within the next few years fortunes will be made in Grand Island lands as well as in those of Buffalo and other sections of the mainland. With the increased demand for manufacturing sites, industrial enterprises will certainly seek that portion of the island nearest to Buffalo and Tonawanda, and the other side, facing Canada, will continue to be occupied by summer resorts, club-houses and residences.

CONCLUSION.

In this little volume an effort has been made to acquaint the reader with the splendid present and the glorious future of Buffalo.

Among the great events in the history of industrial enterprises the turning of Niagara's water power into electric force is one of the most portentous.

A vast field, teeming with wealth, lies open to our view, and the tremendous possibilities — nay, the certainties — for Buffalo are sharply defined. If one tunnel can be constructed, so can two, or a dozen, or a score. Power will keep pace with the demand for it — power cheaper than any other on the face of the earth — and, as it can be easily transmitted, it will be chiefly used where it can be best used, and that is, where the acme of shipping facilities is found and must always concentrate, in Buffalo. The thunder of the Niagara will remain where the waters leap, but its swift lightning is Buffalo's.

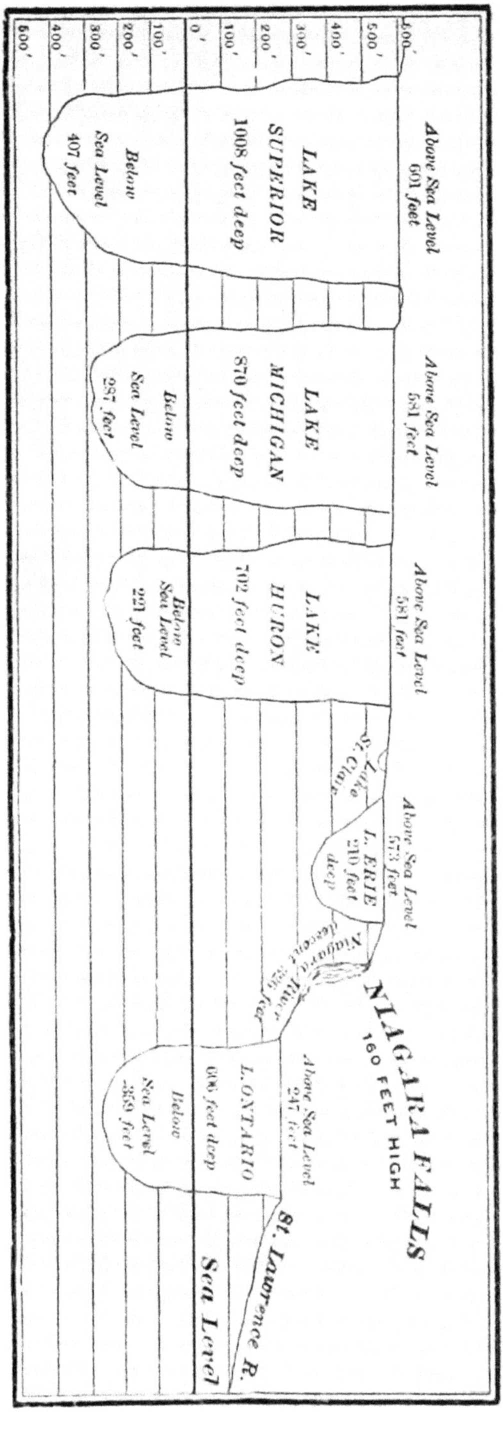

NIAGARA FALLS
160 FEET HIGH

Above Sea Level
601 feet
LAKE
SUPERIOR
1008 feet deep
Below
Sea Level
407 feet

Above Sea Level
581 feet
LAKE
MICHIGAN
870 feet deep
Below
Sea Level
287 feet

Above Sea Level
581 feet
LAKE
HURON
702 feet deep
Below
Sea Level
221 feet

Lake
St. Clair

Above Sea Level
573 feet
L. ERIE
210 feet
deep

Niagara River
descent 326 feet

Above Sea Level
247 feet
L. ONTARIO
606 feet deep
Below
Sea Level
359 feet

St. Lawrence R.

Sea Level

600′
500′
400′
300′
200′
100′
0′
100′
200′
300′
400′
500′

www.ingramcontent.com/pod-product-compliance
Ingram Content Group UK Ltd.
Pitfield, Milton Keynes, MK11 3LW, UK
UKHW020421250726
13967UKWH00007B/2759